# BALDUR AND THE MISTLETOE

Eight hundred years ago, Snorri Sturluson, a chieftain and scholar of Iceland, collected ancient story poems of his people and put them together in a book which we know as *The Younger Edda.* These stories told of the Norse gods whom the Vikings loved. The Vikings were a warrior race and longed to die fighting, for they believed that after their last battle, warriors were carried straight to Valhalla, a golden palace in Asgard, city of the gods. There the Vikings, like the old gods, would fight and feast forever. But as time passed, stories were told of a new young god, Baldur, a god of love and peace. This is his story.

# BALDUR
## AND THE
# MISTLETOE

## A MYTH OF THE VIKINGS

Retold by MARGARET HODGES

Illustrated by GERRY HOOVER

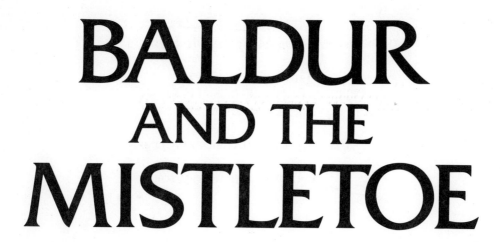

LITTLE, BROWN AND COMPANY
BOSTON                    TORONTO

*Myths of the World*
*Retold by Margaret Hodges*

THE GORGON'S HEAD

THE FIRE BRINGER

PERSEPHONE AND THE SPRINGTIME

BALDUR AND THE MISTLETOE

ILLUSTRATIONS COPYRIGHT © 1974 BY GERRY A. HOOVER

TEXT COPYRIGHT © 1974 BY MARGARET HODGES

FIRST EDITION

T   03/74

Library of Congress Cataloging in Publication Data

Hodges, Margaret.
  Baldur and the mistletoe.

  (Her Myths of the world)
  SUMMARY: Baldur, a young norse god, is protected
from all things except mistletoe.
  Based on the Norse myths contained in The younger
Edda.
  [1. Mythology, Norse]  I.  Hoover, Gerry, illus.
II.  Edda Snorra Sturlusonar.  III.  Title.
IV.  Title: A myth of the vikings.
PZ8.1.H69Bal        293'.2'11        73-608
ISBN 0-316-36787-7

*Published simultaneously in Canada*
*by Little, Brown & Company (Canada) Limited*

PRINTED IN THE UNITED STATES OF AMERICA

*For Fletcher*
*who danced with me*
*in the streets of Reykjavik*


Skoal! to the Northland, skoal!
— *Henry Wadsworth Longfellow*

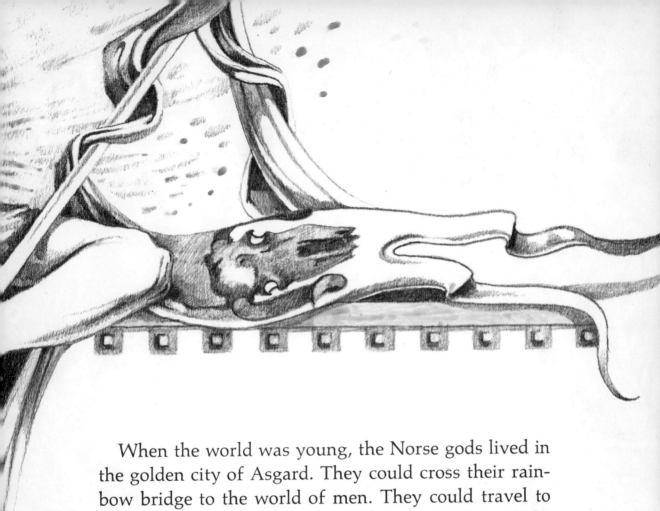

When the world was young, the Norse gods lived in the golden city of Asgard. They could cross their rainbow bridge to the world of men. They could travel to the land of the frost giants and mountain giants. The gods could even reach the place of eternal ice and snow, the place of the dead. But no god wished to leave Asgard.

Brightest and best of all the gods was Baldur. Kind and beautiful, he was loved by gods and men. He understood the meaning of letters and the uses of healing herbs. His sweet wife Nanna loved him better than life. His blind brother Hoder followed him like a fond shadow. Only Loki, the mischief-maker, was jealous of Baldur and longed to destroy him.

One night Baldur dreamed that he must soon leave Asgard. The next night and the next, he dreamed that he saw Hela, goddess of death, preparing her dark palace for some honored guest. He saw the whole world weeping — just as autumn mist and rain weep for the death of summer. Baldur awoke pale and sad. He told his dreams to Frigga, his mother, and to Odin, his father, the all-wise.

There was only one way to learn whether Baldur's dream spoke the truth. Odin mounted his eight-legged horse and left the golden towering palace of Valhalla. From Asgard, he took an untraveled road toward the northern ice. He heard the scream of sea gulls blown in from a stormy sea. He saw the black volcanic land, formed long ago by the hands of giants. Its mountains were crowned with snow that shone like gold under the diamond-bright sun.

Odin galloped on until he came to the land of eternal night, where the snow lies always. And he heard the rivers of Hel roaring. He saw Hel's misty hall, prepared for a feast. The benches were strewn with rings of gold, rich gifts for the expected guests. The tables also were spread with gold. Shields hung upon the wall. And Odin knew that these things were done to honor the coming of Baldur.

Sorrowfully Odin returned to Asgard. But Frigga met him with joyful looks.

"I have saved Baldur," she said. "All things that touch the earth have promised never to harm our son. Fire will not burn him. Water will not drown him. Neither stones, nor iron nor any other metal will cut or bruise him. No sickness, no poison will ever touch him. Trees and all creeping things have sworn the oath. See, the gods have gathered to prove that it is true."

Odin saw Baldur standing before the golden pillars
of Valhalla with the other gods around him. Some, in
play, threw spears at Baldur. Others cast stones and
axes. Nothing hurt Baldur. Stones fell at his feet.
Spears and axes turned aside when they came near him.
Unharmed, Baldur's brightness and beauty shone forth,
and all the gods rejoiced. All, except the jealous Loki.

Loki took the form of an old woman clad in black, her face cold and white as snow. The woman went to Frigga's palace, saying, "The gods will surely kill your son."

"Never," said Frigga. "All things have sworn an oath not to harm Baldur."

"All things?" asked the old woman.

"All things that touch the earth," answered Frigga. "Only the mistletoe did not swear. It grows on a tree to the west of Asgard. The mistletoe does not touch the earth and has no strength of its own. It is too young to take an oath and too weak to hurt Baldur."

At once, the woman turned away. Loki took his own form again and searched until he found the mistletoe, its tiny waxen berries half hidden under the branches of a great oak tree. With a golden scythe he cut down the mistletoe and caught it in a napkin. Then he returned to the gathering of the gods and made his way to blind Hoder, who stood alone outside the circle.

"Why do you not honor Baldur?" said Loki. "You too should throw something to prove that he cannot be hurt."

"I cannot see him," Hoder answered, "and I have no weapon."

Then Loki made an arrow of the mistletoe and sharpened the point. He breathed upon it and the tender stem became hard. He put the dart into the hand of Hoder. "Take my arrow," said Loki. "I will guide your hand."

Straight flew the arrow, and Baldur the Beautiful fell dead, shot through the heart. The light faded from Asgard. The earth grew cold and still. Water turned to ice. Trees dropped their leaves. In the bare branches, birds no longer sang. And in the dark world of the dead, Hela greeted the spirit of her long-expected guest.

Broken with grief, Hoder begged to take Baldur's place in Hel, and Frigga sent Hermod, the messenger, on Odin's horse to ask how Baldur might be released. Like a flash of lightning Hermod sped downward from Asgard until he reached Hel's high gates. There he set spurs to his horse, and leaped the gates into the kingdom of death.

After three days Hermod returned to Asgard with a word of hope. "Hela has said that if all things weep for Baldur, he may go free."

Frigga sent Hermod and all her messengers over the world to ask for tears, and everywhere tears fell. But Hermod, returning again to Asgard, came to a forest of iron trees. There in a deep and rocky cavern sat a hag, bent with age, her face hidden by a rough cloak.

"The spirit of Baldur the Beautiful is held prisoner in Hel until all things on earth shall weep for him," said the messenger. "I ask for your tears."

The old woman gave a loud laugh. "Let Hela keep what she has." From under the cloak gleamed the malicious eyes of Loki.

So, because there was one pair of dry eyes, Baldur the Beautiful could not return to Asgard. Nanna said nothing. Wrapped in silent sorrow, she held her dear lord in her arms, and so fell asleep. Frigga by a kind, swift stroke separated Nanna's spirit from her body and set it free to follow the spirit of Baldur.

For twelve days and nights the gods labored to prepare a worthy funeral. On the seashore they found Baldur's longship, greatest of all ships, and brought logs from the forest to heap upon it. They placed Baldur in his shining armor on the pyre with the gentle Nanna by his side. Gods and giants watched and wondered as Odin knelt and whispered a word into the ear of his dead son. Then with a torch he kindled the fire.

The giants gave a mighty thrust which sent the ship far out on the waves. The flames rose higher and higher as if they would set fire to heaven itself, and the black water shone like molten gold. At last the brilliance faded to a glow of embers. On the far horizon, Baldur's burning ship sank beneath the waves, and darkness again covered the sea.

With the death of Baldur came the Twilight of the Gods. Ages passed and Baldur never returned. Then Time swept away the old gods and the giants in one last battle with Loki and his evil powers. Loki too was destroyed. The ramparts of Asgard fell, worlds crashed in ruin, and the universe was no more. But out of chaos and dark night a new heaven and a new earth were born. In the sky, day dawned again, as bright as the smile of Baldur the Beautiful.

In northern lands, winter still brings a long darkness. But when the sun seems to have gone forever and the mistletoe hangs on the bough, men remember Baldur. Then they light their fires and live in the belief that Baldur will come again. For the word that Odin had whispered was "Hope."